30 DAYS OF TRANSFORMATION
"From the Sideline..."

Kim M. Martin, CATCC

Copyright © 2015 by Kim M. Martin, CTACC
All rights reserved.

ISBN-10: 0692607412
ISBN-13: 978-0692607411

DEDICATION

THIS BOOK IS DEDICATED TO THOSE WHO
UNDERSTAND AND EMBRACE
ROMANS 12:2 WHICH SAYS:

*"AND BE NOT CONFORMED TO THIS WORLD:
BUT BE YE TRANSFORMED BY THE RENEWING
OF YOUR MIND, THAT YE MAY PROVE WHAT
IS THAT GOOD, AND ACCEPTABLE,
AND PERFECT, WILL OF GOD."*

ACKNOWLEDGEMENTS

I would like to thank Jerrod Raymond for always supporting me and being my foundation. You always challenge me to be better and I have graciously accepted the challenge…sometimes…
I love you infinity.

Thank you John and Marie Martin. You are the best parents a child could ever have. You love me unconditionally and have always been there, helping to adjust my wings so I can fly higher.
I love you infinity.

To my lovely daughter Kristine Simmons. You came into my life and gave it meaning. These legacies I leave for you, so you will always know who you are and who you belong to. Continue to shine and know that I am proud of the beautiful woman you are.
I love you infinity

To my business partner and sister-friend for life, Sheronda Barksdale. We have come a long way! Thank you for your faith in me and for being a part of this tremendous transition and transformation in my life. I could not and would not have wanted to do this without you. We've only just begun. The best is yet to come!
I love you infinity.

To all of my friends, collaborators, brothers and sisters in Christ and all of those who have prayed for me and supported me in all that I have envisioned to achieve, I thank you. You have let me know that my work is not in vain.
For that, I love you infinity
Keep watching…
I'm not done…

TABLE OF CONTENTS

Day 1 – Be Ye Transformed… 1
Day 2 – Mind, Body, Spirit… 3
Day 3 – Say Cheese… 5
Day 4 – Good Vibrations 7
Day 5 – And…Action… 9
Day 6 – Owning Your Truth… 11
Day 7 – Self-Care 13
Day 8 – Transformative Learning…................... 15
Day 9 – Misplaced Value… 17
Day 10 – Self-Awareness 19
Day 11 – Girl On Fire… 21
Day 12 – Commitment 23
Day 13 – It's My Time 25
Day 14 – Don't Quit… 28
Day 15 – My Burden is Light 30
Day 16 – Practice Makes…Better… 32
Day 17 – My Flow 34
Day 18 – Be Intentional… 36

Day 19 – Share Your Gifts 38
Day 20 – It Is What It Is… 40
Day 21 – Weight Loss………………………………… 43
Day 22 – Peace… 45
Day 23 – Mosaically You………………………………47
Day 24 – The Power of Connecting… 49
Day 25 – Roots 51
Day 26 – Don't Give That Life 53
Day 27 – Recalibrated…………………………………55
Day 28 – C.O.P.E 57
Day 29 – Fulfillment 59
Day 30 – Unlimited Love & Life… 61
References………………………………………………66

DAY 1
BE YE TRANSFORMED

Romans 12:2 says, *"And be not conformed to this world: but be ye transformed by the renewing of your mind, that ye may prove what is that good, and acceptable, and perfect, will of God."* What a blessing to be transformed! To live with a spirit that has been renewed and refreshed! Behold, all things are new…

Congratulations! At this point, you have been inspired to make changes in your life, you have transitioned through those changes, and are finally living your newly transformed life. Your path is set and your foot is steady. You are walking in your destiny. You have chosen to live your life authentically and have taken full ownership of the decisions you have made. Those around you have begun to take notice. They see a change in you and no longer question your choices, but want to know what you are doing differently. They sense a peace about you. A joy that comes with being fulfilled. They desire to know your "secret" to happiness.

Living a life that is transformative is not always easy and is far from perfect. It is a daily practice. You still may have minor setbacks every once and a while, but the renewing of your mind allows you to handle those situations in a new way. This is yet another part of your journey. Prayerfully it will be one that is filled with experiences of mindfulness and abundance.

Kim's Coaching Corner

Try this exercise in transforming your mind:

Recall an experience in your past when you overcame fear. What did you do to overcome your fear? Do you continue to do things you once feared? How do you handle fear now?

_____
_____
_____
_____
_____
_____
_____

When you reflect on how you overcame fears and what it felt like, it gives you the tools you need to face new challenges fearlessly.

DAY 2
MIND, BODY & SPIRIT

When you begin to live a transformed life, you will seek to align your mind, body and spirit. You will desire to have peace in your life. You will find yourself becoming more mindful of your words and actions. You will become more aware of the importance of taking care of your body and your overall health. Most of all, you will seek a deeper connection spiritually and seek ways in which to honor your Creator. Having these things in alignment will give you an overall sense of wellness and wholeness.

Mindfulness plays a big part in living your transformed life. When we take the time to be mindful of our daily activities, we begin to better understand why we do the things we do. Have you ever gone someplace and can't recall how you got there? There are so many things we do automatically, that we take for granted and no longer appreciate the things we once payed close attention to. This begins to manifest in our lives and can cause us to be dismissive.

As we transform we begin to see the familiar, as though it were unfamiliar again. We gain a fresh perspective and begin to see things we hadn't seen before. We gain a new appreciation for the things around us. It increases our desire to slow down a bit and express gratitude for our blessings. The more cognizant we are of the things going on around us, the more in tune we will be with our minds, bodies and spirit.

Kim's Coaching Corner

Try this exercise in mindfulness:

Prepare yourself for work or school. Take the time to be mindful of all of the steps you take in preparing yourself up until the time you walk out the front door. Answer the following questions:

What was the third thing you did in your preparation for work or school?
_____

How many times did you walk up and down the hallway? _____
Which shoe do you stick your foot in first? _____
How many lights did you turn off before you left the house? _____
Where are your house/car keys kept? _____

Try making it a habit of being mindful, by raising your level of awareness in the day-to-day activities you engage in.

DAY 3
SAY CHEESE!

I have been told on several occasions that I am very photogenic. When my friends complain about not liking how they look in pictures, I always say, "The camera only takes a picture of what it sees!" The lighting may be poor or the picture may come out blurry, but the camera will always capture what it sees. When the user of the camera makes the proper adjustments, the picture comes into focus and what was meant to be captured is clearly seen.

This is true when it comes to how others see us. As we transform, how others see us may change. Is the way you present yourself to others, representative of who you are, or do people still see remnants of the old you? When you transform your mind and begin to live in your truth, the transformation that started within you, begins to reflect outwardly. Others will begin to notice a difference, not only in your actions, but through your facial expressions and body language. The lens that others used to view you through, now displays a sharper and clearer picture of who you are.

As you transform, there will be those who continue to view you the way they used to. Realize that they may be viewing you through their own distorted lens and the adjustment may be theirs to make. When you walk in your truth, you will find yourself liking what you see.

Kim's Coaching Corner

Write down some of the things you believe you have done in the last 3 months that have changed how others view you.

_____
_____
_____
_____

Write down some things you feel you need to do so that others can get a sharper and clearer picture of who you are.

_____
_____
_____
_____

How we present ourselves will determine what role we will play in other people's lives.

DAY 4
GOOD VIBRATIONS

Stephen Bancarz says, "Our dominant thoughts, our physical health, our emotions, and our beliefs all collectively contribute to the vibrational state of our energy field." When we are in alignment, mind, body and spirit, we become centered and our energy "vibration" increases. There are activities we can engage in on a daily basis to raise our vibrations and bring us inner peace. Meditation is a wonderful way to increase your energy vibration. Taking time out your day to be in a meditative state, even if it's just for a few minutes, allows you to just BE as you relax your mind and your body. Conscious breathing is another way to raise our vibration. Taking deep, restorative breaths releases stress and tension.

Laughter, not only releases endorphins, it breaks the tension in any situation and lightens your mood. Your vibrations heighten even higher when you can laugh at yourself and learn to not take things so seriously. Lastly, and this is one of my favorites, live a life of gratitude. The more we learn to appreciate all of the blessings we have, the higher and more frequent our good vibrations will be.

Kim's Coaching Corner

Try this exercise in raising your energy vibration:

Take 3 deep conscious breaths. As you breathe, take time to be aware of how your breath enters and leaves your body. As you inhale, feel the air as it passes through your nostrils, and follow it as it goes down your throat and fills your lungs and diaphragm. As you exhale, feel all of the toxins and stressors as they are released and exit your body. How did you feel after taking those breath? Did you feel "lighter"? Did you experience an increase in your vibrations?

_____
_____
_____
_____

Explore different ways to raise your energy vibrations and make them a part of your daily routine.

DAY 5
AND...ACTION!

My favorite quote is by Benjamin Franklin and it says, "Well done is better than well said". When you choose to live a transformed life, you are choosing to live a life of action. You were willing to act on your desire to discover your passion and purpose. You were willing to make transitions in your life so that you could live out that passion and purpose. You have accepted the call to action.

Each day when you wake up and think about or write down your intentions for the day, you are creating an action plan. Your plan is to successfully accomplish those goals, so that you can create new ones. Each day has purpose, and you are driven by it. Your purpose is to make a difference in your life and the lives of others, with God getting the glory.

Your actions don't just involve movement. They involve the way you act. When you live a transformed life, you act out of love and respect for others. You begin to see the good in others as well.

You desire is to protect, inspire and empower those around you, as well as yourself. It is a sign that you have truly transformed.

Kim's Coaching Corner

Try this exercise in living a life of action:

Every morning, take the time to write down your intentions for the day. This will assist you in carrying out your goals for the day, and also holds you accountable for prioritizing and managing your time.
What are your intentions for today?

1. _____
2. _____
3. _____
4. _____
5. _____

Writing down your intentions is your course of action for the day.
Be purpose driven.

DAY 6
OWNING YOUR TRUTH

Living a transformed life means owning it. You make no apologies for who you are or the decisions you make. The confidence you exude is not cocky or self-centered. It comes from your ability to embrace your beliefs and live in your truth.

In order to own your transformed life, you have to be fearless and willing to defend what you believe, even if it is not popular or readily accepted by others. Owning your truth may end relationships you thought were secure, because you have chosen to be honest with yourself about what you want and need. You ultimately learn to be comfortable in your own skin and it feels good!

Owning who you are is a responsibility that should not be taken lightly. You are representing who you are and that representation comes with integrity. Loving and owning who you are, also means loving and respecting others for who they are as well. With that being said, OWN RESPONSIBLY!

Kim's Coaching Corner

Try this exercise in owning it:

Think about something that you firmly believe in. Now, write down what that belief is and how you own it. How do you react when someone challenges that belief?

_____
_____
_____
_____
_____

Owning who you are means you are unashamed of who you are and not afraid to defend it.

DAY 7
SELF-CARE

The beauty of living a transformed life is that you have learned to take care of YOU. You have a heightened sense of awareness when it comes to responding to your own needs. You not only listen to your body, but respond to it positively, so it is refreshed and restored. You have learned to put YOU first.

There is no harm in putting yourself first. You understand that you cannot be the vessel God called to be, if you don't take care of yourself. Think about the way you take care of your car or your home. You take your car in for tune-ups and oil changes and put gas in it so that you can safely transport yourself, your friends and your family. You take care of your home and make any necessary repairs to ensure that it is a safe place for you and your family to reside. We must do the same with our bodies, minds and spirits. They need to be "tuned-up" in order for us to be our best.

More importantly, we have to be aware of the signs that alert us when self-care is necessary. It is not something that should be ignored. We should give ourselves the care we need with as much urgency as we do a flat tire or faulty plumbing. We only have one body. We need to treat it with love and respect so it will serve us and those who need us. Our body is our temple. Treat it well.

> *Kim's coaching corner*
>
> *Try this exercise in self-care:*
>
> *Write down at least two things you do on a regular basis to take care of your mind, body and spirit.*
>
> *Mind:_____,_____*
> *Body:_____,_____*
> *Spirit:_____, _____*
>
> *Have you been able to identify the signs that let you know you are in need of self-care? When you do, respond to them quickly and with care.*

DAY 8
TRANSFORMATIVE LEARNING

The beauty of living a transformed life is the growth that takes place. With the renewing of your mind, comes a bit of a learning curve. There is a paradigm shift that takes place in your life and you become exposed to new experiences. As you transform, you will experience transformative learning.

Transformative learning involves taking a critical look at the beliefs and assumptions we have had in the past and making conscious steps to change them to create a better future. While experiencing transformative learning, we are changing some of the thoughts and attitudes that have been with us, as a part of our belief system, for a long time. With that, comes vulnerability, but a willingness to exchange old ways for new ones. It is a process that changes our outlook about ourselves, our relationships and how we view the world.

We gain this knowledge through reading, researching and connecting with those who are knowledgeable about the things we have questions about. Once we discover the answers and find them sufficient, we begin to walk in that truth. Any time new questions arise, we return to this way of learning knowing that we will find the answers what we seek.

Kim's Coaching Corner

Try this exercise in transformational thinking:

Think about a belief that you had in the past and have since changed. Was it against a race or religion? Was is something that you believed about yourself? What was it that changed your mindset?

_____
_____
_____
_____
_____
_____

Transformative learning is an ongoing process that allows us to live peacefully in our truth.

DAY 9
MISPLACED VALUE

Oscar Wilde has been quoted as saying, "We know the cost of everything, but the value of nothing". There are things in our lives we place value on that we shouldn't. One thing we should be able to ask ourselves is: Will who we are be diminished if we were to lose this thing we place value in? If the answer is no, then we may need to let it go. Letting go can be more powerful than trying to defend or hang on to something that takes us out of alignment with who we are.

Living a transformed life helps us put the things we value into perspective. The material things we possess no longer have the level of valuation they once had. We learn to be grateful for what we have been given stewardship over, and take care of it accordingly. If they were taken away, we understand that it does not affect the person we are or what we represent. We may even be prompted to give what we have away because our abundance and fulfillment is not found in those items, but in other areas of our life.

What we begin to value is our value system; those principles and standards we choose to live by. That value system, if lost, would diminish who we are. Living a transformed life frees us from misplaced value and allows us to embrace the true value system that makes us whole.

Kim's Coaching Corner

Try this exercise in identifying misplaced value:

What is something you have given up that you once placed value in? How did you feel once that item was gone? Are there more things that you feel you need to let go of?

_____
_____
_____
_____
_____

Releasing things we once thought were valuable, allows us to see that we are not defined by what we have, but who we are.

DAY 10
SELF-AWARENESS

The dictionary defines self-awareness as the ability to recognize oneself as an individual separate from the environment and other individuals. Self-awareness involves a higher level of consciousness that allows us to pay attention to our thoughts and feelings in the present moment. We are able to focus in on the things going on around us and how we choose to respond to them.

We learn to better identify our strengths and weaknesses. We learn what truly motivates us. We understand our thoughts and beliefs and the impact they have on us and the interactions we have with others. We can look ahead and see our future, based on how we choose to respond in our present. Our emotions, behavior and the way we talk to others is enhanced because of this level of self-awareness.

Self-awareness allows us to change the direction of our lives because we learning to interpret and master our emotions. With time and practice, it becomes intuitive. It is a practice that can truly transform us.

Kim's Coaching Corner

Try this exercise in awareness:

Sit comfortably in a chair or lie down. Close your eyes. Imagine yourself stepping out of your body. Can you see yourself with your mind's eye? What do you see?

_____
_____
_____
_____
_____

Being aware allows you to focus on yourself and the things going on around you with a new sense of clarity.

DAY 11
GIRL ON FIRE

In the words of Alicia Keys, "This girl is on fire!" Each one of us has a small flame inside of us. It is our motivation and our desire to carry out our vision for our lives. It is our inspiration, and has always lived within us.

It was smoldering because of past hurts, beliefs and negative thoughts of who we were. It almost went out because of fear and doubt that we could not achieve our visions and aspirations. It was almost forgotten due to the toxic relationships we were in that served as a distraction.

When we learn to live a transformed life, we learn what motivates us and keeps that flame burning strong. Love for ourselves and the desire to positively affect the lives of others, fuels that fire. If that flame begins to flicker, those in your inner circle provide the kindling we need to keep going. The flame may flicker from time to time, but it never completely goes out. It burns eternal. When we are on fire, there is nothing we can't do! Our flames don't burn others. It refines them with love. What is left is the afterglow…

Kim's Coaching Corner

Try this exercise in being a "girl on fire":

Read Chapter 3 of the book of Daniel in the Bible. It is the story of Shadrach, Meshach, and Abednego. Write down how this story applies to your personal transformation.

_____
_____
_____
_____
_____

Keeping your internal flame lit will deflect those things trying to extinguish it.

DAY 12
COMMITMENT

Your journey to living a transformed life started with your commitment. Your commitment to acting on what inspired you. Your commitment to taking the leap of faith and transitioning toward your passion and purpose. Your commitment to renewing your mind in order be transformed. You weren't casual about making a change in your life. You were intentional and committed!

There are so many things we want for our lives, that we simply haven't been willing to commit to. We wanted the high- paying job, the big house and the meaningful relationship, but we didn't want to do the work or put in the time necessary to earn it. When we expect others to commit and we don't reciprocate, we can't expect to experience the manifestation that comes along with our commitment.

Living a transformed life means making a commitment to change. A commitment to change how we think and react to the events that take place in our lives. A commitment to loving ourselves and others for who we are. It means being committed to investing in ourselves, so we can be the vessels we were destined to. A

a result of our commitment, the manifestation and harvest will come.

Kim's Coaching Corner

Try this exercise in being committed:

Write down an area in your life that you feel may be lacking the level of commitment you desire. How will you go about re-committing yourself?
_____
_____
_____
_____
_____

Commit to being the best YOU you can be!

DAY 13
IT'S MY TIME

Author and poet, Geoffrey Chaucer, said this famous quote, "Time and tide waits for no man". We will never have the ability to stop the passage of time. We have been given 24 hours to complete tasks and to create the balance we desire in our lives. That's 1,140 minutes…86,400 seconds. It is our time to do with as we see fit.

In this world of advanced technology, we have been conditioned to believe that we have to be accessible to everyone at all times. As soon as or phone rings or a notification tone chimes, we abruptly stop what we are doing and scramble for our phones, not wanting to miss someone trying to connect with us. But what about when we need time to connect with ourselves?

When I am meditating or exercising, I silence my phone or leave it in another area of my home. The purpose of that time is to center myself and to move my body WITHOUT interruption. I am preparing myself to be the best me I can be for the day, and I don't want that time interrupted. Whatever calls come in, have to wait. When I am done, then I can respond with a clear mind or react with renewed energy. If I am constantly making myself available at all times, I am not respecting my time with myself. If I don't value my time, I can't expect others to. I have to ensure that I am being the best steward of my time, because I can't get that time back.

When living a transformed life, you learn the importance of being present in all of the interactions and connections you have with others. When you set appointments, you remove things that will distract you, so that you experience the fullness of the time you set aside to be with that person. When you feel that you can't give your full attention or your best, you either reschedule or say you can't meet with them because you have learned the importance of their time too. Your focus is on reaping the benefits of being able to fully engage and be filled by the experience. Time and tide waits for no man. Continue to learn to use it wisely.

Kim's Coaching Corner

Try this exercise in owning your time:

Write down your intentions for the day (your "to-do" list). Next to those intentions, write down approximately how long each task should take to complete. At the end of the day, look at your list. Were you able to complete everything? What interruptions or distractions took place? How did you respond to them?

_____
_____
_____
_____
_____

Owning your time and how it is spent adds meaning and depth to your life's experiences. Make no apologies for how you spend it.

DAY 14
DON'T QUIT

When you take the big leap to follow your passion and your purpose, you may find that things don't manifest the way you anticipated. During this time, you may even revert back to your old way of thinking. Doubt and fear may even step out of the dark corners of your mind in an attempt to reclaim their thrones in your life. In your frustration, you may want to throw up your hands and exclaim, "I quit!"

Just because we have chosen to live a transformed life, doesn't mean that we will no longer face obstacles. It does not mean that we are exempt from attempts to be "wronged" or mistreated. What it means is that we now have the tools necessary to handle things better and those negative experiences are now fewer and further between. When they do arise, and we haven't experienced them in a while, our carnal instinct is to react and respond the way we used to. This is where we have to be mindful enough to realize that we may be overreacting, and aware enough to stop, assess our emotions and determine the best solution to the problem.

Living a life of transformation exposes us to all of our emotional truths. Even those that make us want to quit. With time and practice, we will learn to allow those feelings to flow through us so we can move forward in our journey toward personal growth and success.

Kim's Coaching Corner
Try this exercise not quitting:

Start a gratitude journal. At the end of each day, write down three things you are grateful for. Read through your journal periodically to remind you of the small blessings that have taken place in your life.

_____
_____
_____
_____
_____

Expressing gratitude affirms the positive and encourages us to press on!

DAY 15
MY BURDEN IS LIGHT

The beauty of living a transformed life is that you begin to feel "lighter". The pain of past toxic relationships, fear, anxiety and stress no longer weigh on your mind or your body. They have been replaced with joy, a sense of well-being and inner peace. The passion and purpose you once craved, is being manifested, leaving you feeling energized.

Living a transformed life creates in you a level of awareness that helps identify those emotional burdens that kept you feeling oppressed and immobile. You learn to let those feelings flow through you and not reside in you. The weight from harboring those negative thoughts and feelings has been lifted.

When we receive information, whether positive or negative, we have the choice to either accept it with gratitude, or release it. Feelings of guilt can make us hold on to emotional baggage longer than we need to. "Lightness" comes when we can cast our burdens of guilt shame and inadequacy aside and stand boldly in who we are.

Kim's Coaching Corner

Try this exercise in lightening your burden:

Fill a backpack with 3-5 cans from your pantry. Wear that backpack for a few hours as you go about your day. How did it affect you physically and emotionally? How did you feel when you finally took it off?

_____
_____
_____
_____
_____
_____

*Releasing emotional baggage leaves you
feeling emotionally and spiritually lighter.*

DAY 16
PRACTICE MAKES...BETTER

Living a transformed life takes practice. Being able to live in a state of mindfulness and awareness can be difficult, especially when there are so many things that stimulate and distract us. Our lives may never be perfect, but they can be better. Studies have shown that it takes, on average, 21 days to create a habit. Quite honestly, the habits that we create manifest from two sources; our commitment to change and the strategy that we choose to make that change. If we are not willing to commit to the change or don't have a solid strategy for making the change, we are setting ourselves up for failure.

If we are going to live a transformed life, we have to practice living that way. It does not happen overnight and it is not easily maintained. It is a process. It requires having the mental and physical tools that we need to respond to our thoughts and emotions as they come. It is an exercise in determining what works best for you. Without practice, we may find ourselves falling back into old routines and thoughts. Our willingness to practice and apply those things that will transform us, will lead to a more fulfilled and abundant life.

Kim's Coaching Corner

Try this exercise in practicing good habits:

Think about something that you want to achieve in the next 21 days. Write down how you plan to accomplish this. Write down your start date. In 21 days, write down whether you were successful or not. What do you believe caused you to succeed or not? Was there something you could have done differently?

_____
_____
_____
_____
_____
_____

*Practice those habits and behaviors you want for your life.
It starts with your commitment and a solid plan.*

DAY 17
MY FLOW

Your flow is the series of events you pass through from the time you initiate something, until the time it is complete.

Your flow is your personal style and how you choose to do what you do. It's what makes you unique. We all may have similar situations, but we all have a different flow in how we deal with them.

Your flow is your journey. It started with inspiration, which began the transition to your transformation. In our experiences, we will have ebbs and flows. There will be times where we will experience highs and lows, times of happiness and sorrow. They were intended to help us transform into the person we need to be. So, "check your flow". Allow others to see how you do things and respect how they do things as well. They will either vibe with you or be turned off. The beauty is that your flow is authentically yours.

As you grow and expand, you will experience changes in how you flow. You will find that your flow is more fluid, the more aligned you are with who you've become. Your life flow will transform into your life force…

Kim's Coaching Corner

Try this exercise in identifying your flow:

Write down those things you feel differentiate you from anybody else. What are those things you believe make you unique (your clothing style, your hair, the way you walk, how you interact with others, etc.)? Describe how you flow?

_____
_____
_____
_____
_____
_____

Check your flow. It should represent the authentic you!

DAY 18
BE INTENTIONAL

As you live your transformed life, you become more intentional about the things you do. This is because you know the "why" behind the things you do. You are not doing things with "good intentions" as a means of being self-serving. You understand that there are consequences for the decisions you make and you are choosing to make those decisions with your eyes wide open.

When we do things intentionally, they are done on purpose and deliberately. They are planned and thought out. The key is ensuring that your intentions don't harm others or justify you doing things that are morally wrong. You have defined your values and are doing things intentionally based on those values. Being intentional about what you do is not always comfortable, but you know that it is necessary in order to live a transformative life. You are choosing to be proactive, and not reactive in your behavior or actions.

Being intentional means that you choose to do those things that are best for you. You have taken the time to observe, research and listen to those around you, gleaned what you felt was beneficial, and are now intentional about carrying out the decisions you have made. You have finally reached the place of living your life's purpose, ON purpose.

Kim's Coaching Corner

Try this exercise in living intentionally by answering the following questions:

1. *When I do things with intent, I feel*
   _____
   _____
   _____
   _____

2. *If I am more intentional about the things I say and do, then I will*
   _____
   _____
   _____
   _____

Be deliberate about your intentions.
They should be in alignment with your value and your vision.

DAY 19
SHARE YOUR GIFTS

From the moment that our father's seed was planted in our mother's egg, we were given a gift. We were given the gift of life. We were given an opportunity to come into this world to share the gift of our purpose. We had purpose before we even knew we had purpose. Best of all, we were allowed to go on this beautiful journey of self-discovery in which we identify our gifts and use them to make a difference in the world. It is a precious gift that God has given to us. We are the vessels He made, to bring our gifts to those in need of them.

There are so many people who are out there waiting for us to step into our purpose, so they are positioned to walk into theirs. There are so many people waiting for us to step out on faith and out of our current situation, so they can take our place and step into what is theirs. It is a beautiful circle of life when we are obedient and aware of the shifts we need to make. It creates a joy and fulfillment beyond measure.

Living our transformed life means leaving this world having fulfilled our passion and purpose. Our goal should be to leave this world EMPTY because we gave all that we had and used our gifts to leave a legacy for who will come behind us.

Kim's Coaching Corner

Try this exercise in sharing your gifts:

Write down the ways in which you are actively sharing your gifts. If you aren't, write down some ways that you can start.

_____
_____
_____
_____
_____

Once you identify your gifts, be excited to share them!

DAY 20
IT IS WHAT IT IS

The term, "It is what it is", has irritated me from the moment I heard it. I felt it was a very dismissive term, like when people say, "whatever!" I also felt as though the person who said it was giving up or settling for the situation they were in. I simply did not care for the term. As I became more mindful of the things that were being said to me, my perspective of the term changed. I began to look at the term with regard to acceptance and it took on a whole new meaning.

Dictionary.com defines the word "accept" as "the consent to receive" or "to come to recognize an opinion as correct". Acceptance does not mean that we will like what we receive or that it will be pleasant. When we fully accept those areas of our lives where we know change needs to occur, we release ourselves to begin the healing process and to seek the help we need to overcome that situation. We no longer live in a state of denial.

Living a transformed life means having a level of awareness to accept situations in your life that may be lacking fulfillment. Think about your health. When you have pain, you identify the pain and seek professional help to address it. You don't allow the pain to become intolerable and just dismiss it a though it doesn't exist. Eventually it will consume you and change the quality of your life. The goal should be to identify and resolve the problem.

Think about your relationships. When you are in a toxic relationship and you accept the fact that the relationship is causing you emotional stress and you choose to end it, a tremendous weight is lifted off of you. You no longer feel the stress or responsibility that comes along with being in that relationship. You feel a sense of freedom, and it all started with your willingness to accept the things that are going on in your life. It is what it is. The second and most important step, however, is to do something about it! Transformation is about movement to a space of well-being. That well-being comes from acceptance and your willingness to heal.

Kim's Coaching Corner

Try this exercise in acceptance:

Stand in front of your mirror completely nude. Take the time to look at every part of your body. What do you like or not like about what you see? Write down how you feel about your body and what it means to take a long, hard look at yourself.

_____
_____
_____
_____
_____

Get in the habit of being aware of who you are inside and out.

DAY 21
WEIGHT LOSS

Living a transformed life requires you to lose weight. You may look in the mirror and not see the physical weight melting away, but you still feel lighter. The emotional weight that you carried for so long is gone! The chains of the belief system that you had regarding your self-worth, have been broken. The anchors of doubt and fear, no longer have you "stuck". You have lost emotional weight and it shows!

The weight loss shows in your character. It shows in your energy level. It shows in your overall outlook on life. It shows in the way that you flow. You have swag… and all because your emotional diet has changed. Binging on negative thoughts and craving acceptance from those who don't want to see you grow, have been removed from your emotional menu. You have found balance; the balance of time that allows you to take care of yourself so that you can be fully present with others. You are receiving the nutrients you need from the positive interactions, gratitude and fulfillment you receive each day. Your mind, body and spirit are aligning more and more due to the nourishment that being true to yourself brings.

When we are free from emotional weight loss, the desire to remove physical weight will follow, because our satisfaction won't be found in physical "comfort foods". Our satisfaction will come from the food we feed our souls.

Kim's Coaching Corner

Try this exercise in emotional weight loss:

Think about the one thing that used to really "push your buttons". What practice or method do you use to release the emotional weight?
_____
_____
_____
_____
_____

Exercising awareness will keep us emotionally fit.

DAY 22
PEACE

Deepak Chopra made a very profound statement about peace. He said, "There is no way to peace. Peace IS the way." We seek to have peace once we have completed a goal in our lives. Peace should be sought first. It should be the space that you enter into as you as you set out to accomplish your goals.

When you come from a place of peace, you come in love. You seek to have harmony with those you interact with and see the best in who they are. Judgement and expectation take no root in your spirit. In situations that are emotionally charged, you seek to find a common ground as a means to defuse and not incite anger. Peace isn't the solution, but the foundation by which you live.

Peace is the freedom from disturbance where we experience quietness and tranquility from within. Meditation and centering ourselves brings us into that space of perfect peace. Our transformative life centers around living fully in that peace. Our actions and attitudes will be evident of that peace. Most of all, our life of peace will give reverence to the awesome God we serve.

Kim's Coaching Corner

Try this exercise in living in peace:

Create a time in the morning that can be dedicated to prayer or meditation. It should be a time when you are least likely to be interrupted. Make sure that the space is comfortable and conducive to you being able to center yourself. Start out with a short time frame and increase the time as you are led to. How does this time affect the remainder of your day?

_____
_____
_____
_____
_____

Start your day by operating from a place of peace.

DAY 23
MOSAICALLY YOU

As individuals, we have traits and personalities that make us unique. Our environment, beliefs and experiences, shape our thoughts and create a picture of what we think our lives should be. As we go through life, we may experience negative situations that fragment what we thought was a good.

Our lives can begin to feel like scattered pieces, filled with emotional highs and lows. We may get to a place where we feel broken and we aren't quite sure how to "fix" it. We may not be able to see how the fragmented parts of our lives can be put back together to make us whole again.

Living a transformative life, allows us to take those fragmented pieces of our lives and create a beautiful mosaic. The pieces of our lives come together and bound by self-acceptance, self-value and self-love. What once appeared to be broken, is now seen as complete by those who take the time to marvel at its beauty. We are a light and a reflection of our experiences. Be mosaically you.

Kim's Coaching Corner

Try this exercise in being mosiacally you:

Think about a time in your life when you felt as though your life didn't have much direction. Think about how others may have viewed you during that time. Then, think about your experience as things began to come together. Was their view different? Explain the parallels.

_____
_____
_____
_____
_____

No matter what we experience, we can still be made beautiful and whole.

DAY 24
THE POWER OF CONNECTING

One of my favorite things to say after I meet someone for the first time is, "It was a pleasure connecting with you." When you live a transformative life, the interactions you have with others, take on a new meaning. You don't want to just engage in idle chatter with an individual. You seek to connect with them and experience who they are. You are curious to know what piece of life's puzzle belongs to them and how your pieces may fit together.

Connections are powerful and transform our lives in a radical way. We connect with God through prayer and worship. We connect with ourselves through meditation, awareness and mindfulness. We connect with others through interactions where we focus on being present. All of these methods keep us connected with the purpose of aligning our minds, bodies and spirits. We were not made to be on this earth alone.

We were connected to our mother at our inception. She provided what we needed until we were ready to enter this world. Once the umbilical was broken, it was time for us to connect in a way that would sustain us. We were meant to connect with our God, ourselves and others to create experiences that will restore and replenish us. As you continue to transform, be mindful of the connections you make and the impact they will have on your life.

Kim's Coaching Corner

Try this exercise in connecting:

Think about the ways in which you connect spiritually, emotionally and physically with yourself and those around you. Are you simply going through the motions or are you actively seeking ways in which to truly plug-in and connect with those around you? Write down your thoughts.

_____
_____
_____
_____

Actively seek to make connections that will restore you.

DAY 25

ROOTS

So many of the seeds that have been planted in our spirit have taken root and flourished, because we have given them life. Our emotions have provided the fertile ground necessary for both positive and negative seeds to grow. As with any seed, the more water and light it is given, the stronger the roots become.

When negative things are said to us and we believe them, those beliefs take root inside of us. The longer we accept what is said as the truth, the deeper those roots go and the longer it takes for us to remove them. They become like weeds and try to take over any positive thoughts we may have about ourselves. The desire is to develop a weed killer for those roots that have already been planted and to create a way to keep them from returning. This happens as we transform. Transformation provides the weeding and preparation that our spirits need. It creates new and fertile ground for seeds of greatness to be planted and harvested. As mindfulness and clarity increase, negative thoughts and beliefs decrease and no longer have a space to thrive. The bad seeds may try to take root, but the changes in our lives come in like a fresh wind, simply blowing them away.

Kim's Coaching Corner

Try this exercise in root planting:

As you are transitioning, what positive roots have you planted in your life that are flourishing?

_____
_____
_____
_____
_____

Transformation is the weeding that is done to remove negative seeds from our spirit.

DAY 26
DON'T GIVE THAT LIFE

As you sojourn through your transformed life, there will be situations and individuals that will come along to challenge the peace that you have created in your life. Comments will be made and opportunities may arise that you thought were going to align with your purpose. For a minute you may act out of emotion and respond negatively to the situation. When situations like this try to manifest themselves, we have to be careful not to give them life.

Individuals who make comments that do not edify you, are only seeking attention for themselves. They want to elevate themselves, by repressing who you are. When we focus our attention on what they are trying to do to us, we give them the "life" they need to continue doing it. We give them authority they don't deserve. When situations don't turn out the way we plan and we throw our hands up in defeat, we give that situation "life". We don't glean from it the lessons that needed to be learned.

The only life we should be willing to give ourselves is one that fosters peace, self-acceptance and love. Every now and then, the temptation may arise where we feel the need to defend ourselves. As we continue to transform, what naysayers think or what certain situations may create, will have no significance because our authenticity and purpose will provide the clarity we need to see through those "non-issues" with confidence and ease.

Kim's Coaching Corner

Try this exercise in not giving people or situations "life":

Think about a time when you felt that someone personally attacked your character and you responded negatively to it. How did you feel afterwards? Did it change or confirm that individual's feelings? How would you have handled it differently now?

_____
_____
_____
_____

Give life to things that foster vibrancy and elevation in your life.

DAY 27
RECALIBRATED

There is a workshop that I have created called "RedeFINDing You". The question that I ask all of the participants is, "If you were to place your life in your navigation system, where would it take you? Do you have a clear path for your life or are you constantly in a state of recalculating?" I also speak about having an internal navigation system that needs to be "recalibrated" as we change our way of thinking. The old "maps" (negative thoughts and mindsets) need to be replaced with the new ones as we align ourselves mind, body and spirit. We now see opportunities to take our lives in a different direction.

Recalibration involves a graduation. What worked for us for a long period of time, is no longer producing the results we once thought were good. The area that we currently are in is familiar, but there are some opportunities we missed by remaining stagnant. We reached a place where we were just existing, but not living.

When the recalibration takes place, those things that existed in our lives may remain, but those new avenues and spaces are revealed to us and those things we didn't see before are brought to our awareness. This recalibration can take place many times throughout our lives as we continue to align with our true self. The more mindful we are, the better our chances are of not missing those "updates" as they come.

Kim's Coaching Corner

Try this exercise in recalibrating yourself:

Think of an area in your life where you felt "stuck". What were some to the things that you did to move past that point? What new things have you experienced as a result?

_____
_____
_____
_____
_____

Recalibrate so you can have a clear path toward your life's path and purpose.

DAY 28

C.O.P.E.

Cope is defined as the ability to deal effectively with something difficult. Coping mechanisms were designed to assist you in that effort. Unfortunately, mental, physical and sexual abuse, along with drugs, alcohol and other unhealthy indulgences have taken the effectiveness out of how we deal with difficult situations in our lives.

My business partner Sheronda and I have a program that we offer through our coaching business called C.O.P.E. The acronym stands for Creating Our Peaceful Existence. We believe that our ability to effectively deal with any situation starts with developing the tools necessary for creating a peaceful existence. Coping mechanisms that are problem-solving based help us focus on how we address problems to reduce stress. Emotion-focused coping mechanism give us the tools to nurture our emotional health during stressful times. When we develop those tools, we create a resource that can be accessed whenever we find ourselves in an emotionally stressful situation. When we learn to C.O.P.E., we focus in on loving ourselves and valuing who we are, so we can project that love onto others.

Kim's Coaching Corner

Try this exercise in coping:

Reflect on how you currently deal with negative situations. Is your coping mechanism an effective way to deal with the problem? What are some ways you feel you can create your peaceful existence?

_____
_____
_____
_____
_____

We all have different methods of coping. Be sure that your mechanism promotes positive and effective results.

DAY 29

FULFILLMENT

When we find happiness and peace in our lives, we experience a sense of fulfillment. Fulfillment comes because we are no longer living our lives through our ego. We are living our lives through our souls. We believe that we have everything we need. We no longer measure ourselves by any external standards. We don't fear situations that come our way, because we are at peace. We've learned to love ourselves so completely, and in turn can love others.

When we learn to exist in a space of fulfillment, feelings of frustration, self-judgment, and fear, are replaced with feelings of enthusiasm, inspiration, and joy. The things that we do for ourselves and others are not forced or burdensome. We desire to do things without expectancy. No self-serving thoughts enter our mind. Only that what we are doing comes from a place of pure love.

As we continue to live our transformed lives we have to be mindful that being fulfilled doesn't mean that we will always be happy or joyful. If we are constantly in a state of happiness and we avoid any other emotions, we won't continue to expand and grow. We will still experience sadness, disappointment, frustration and failure, but we are fulfilled because we are WHOLE. We have learned the value of who we are, where we are and where we are "growing".

Kim's Coaching Corner

Try this exercise in being fulfilled:

Think back to a time when you were involved in an activity that you were successful in and had fun doing at the same time? What were you doing and why did it make you feel good. Are there other opportunities for you to do this again? What other gifts do you have to share?

_____
_____
_____
_____
_____
_____

Fulfillment comes when you develop your character from within.

DAY 30
UNLIMITED LOVE & LIFE

My Blog Talk Radio co-host Sheronda Barksdale and I end each of our episodes by saying "Keep Your Love Unlimited". It is the hashtag that we use at the end of our posts on our Facebook and Instagram pages. It is what we want our listeners and followers to do as they go about their life's journey. In all things, we want everyone we connect with to remember that the love and life they live is not limited by the confines that others try to put on them. Their love and life has unlimited possibilities.

As I conclude this final book in my "From the Sideline" series, I am reminded of the journey. From my dear friend Michelle Grant who first encouraged to me write my first book, to my "inner circle" of friends who have walked with me as I went through significant transitions in my life; to my ability to love with my WHOLE heart, the beautiful person I see in the mirror. As I transformed and renewed my mind, I was reminded of one thing. Never forgot to LOVE. Love enough to be inspired. Love enough to walk boldly through transition.

Love enough to transform and renew your mind. Love without limits and fearlessly…

I love this quote by William W. Purkey:

> *Sing like no one is listening.*
>
> *Love like you've never been hurt.*
>
> *Dance like nobody's watching,*
>
> *and live like it's heaven on*
>
> *earth*

Kim's Coaching Corner

Today's call to action is to…

#KEEPYOURLOVEUNLIMITED
Be blessed…

"Breaking the Boundaries of Love and Life"

Visit our website www.unlimitedloveandlife.com

Like Us on Facebook www.facebook.com/unlimitedloveandlife

Follow Us on Twitter www.twitter.com/loveunlimitedco

Follow Us on Instagram www.instagram.com/unlimitedloveandlife

Follow Our Blog Talk Radio Show www.blogtalkradio.com/loveunlimited

Kim M. Martin & Sheronda L. Barksdale are
Life Empowerment Coaches, Authors and
Professional Speakers
They are the Co-Founders of Unlimited Love and Life
Coaching, LLC and the Co-Hosts of the Blog Talk Radio
Show, "Love Unlimited: Relationship Coaching
with Kim and Sheronda"

Visit our website to schedule your coaching session, workshop or public speaking engagement TODAY!

Visit www.amazon.com/author/kimmmartin
to purchase my latest books online

References

http://www.spiritscienceandmetaphysics.com/5-ways-to-raise-your-vibration/#sthash.7bhRqgdv.dpuf

http://www.lifehack.org/articles/productivity/50-ways-live-more-fulfilling-life.html

http://lifeyourway.net/what-does-it-mean-to-live-intentionally/

http://www.mindbodygreen.com/0-9610/how-to-create-a-life-of-true-fulfillment.html

http://www.pathwaytohappiness.com/self-awareness.htm

A New Earth: Create a Better Life by Eckhart Tolle

MindWorks by Gary vanWarmerdam

https://www.semel.ucla.edu/dual-diagnosis-program/News_and_Resources/How_Do_You_Cope

www.ingramcontent.com/pod-product-compliance
Lightning Source LLC
Chambersburg PA
CBHW051705090426
42736CB00013B/2551